Happy fathers da
to

GW01458280

The Making of a Father

Paul Fadeyi

Published by

PaulFadeyi.com

Published by Paul Fadeyi

British Library Cataloguing Data

A catalogue record of this book is available from the British Library

Typesetting and production management by
www.ccdgroup.co.uk

To obtain further copies or contact author:
Website: www.paulfadeyi.com
Email: paul@paulfadeyi.com

Printed in England

Dedication

This book is dedicated to the glory of God the Father. Also, in memory of my late Parents, Pa Moses Folorunso Fadeyi and Madam Florence Taiye Fadeyi for all the moral and spiritual values they taught me from childhood.

Foreword

It gives me great joy to write a foreword to Bishop Paul Kunle Fadeyi's latest book, 'The making of a Father'. Having read previous books by the author, I am particularly happy that he has again chosen a topical subject as the focus of discussion in this latest book.

Most recent discussions about the roles of fathers in our modern societies are often anecdotal and superficial. Indeed, the subject emerges only when tragic behaviours of the younger generation remind us that such perpetrators could be products of faulty homes - where father figures are absent. However, once we recover from the shock of such tragic news, we often slide back to our "usual" life - waiting again for another tragic occurrence to remind us of the dwindling in the number of quality fathers who can make a difference in our spiritual, political and secular life.

I think this attitude exposes us to two potent dangers: first, is the tendency to limit the relevance of "fatherhood" to the provision of leadership that can prevent tragedy; while the other is the propensity to assume that "fatherhood" is just mainly a "family" or "home" event. I think these are both wrong and Bishop Fadeyi's book attested to this. The book goes deep in its analysis of the place of quality Fatherhood in our society. Quite notably, Bishop Fadeyi contends that Fatherhood is a process and not an occurrence; that it requires provision of inspiration, not reliance on control, and that it depends on consensus and not imposition of dictatorship. These are some of the important features of this book.

Bishop Fadeyi is eminently qualified to write a book of this nature. Apart from being the biological father of delightful children, he has been playing the role of spiritual father to the congregation of Grace Outreach Church, a church that started 16 years ago in South East London but has now expanded worldwide, even spreading to those parts of the world where many consider unimaginable.

In conclusion, I consider 'The making of a Father' to be a brilliant treatise of a most topical subject and I believe very strongly that we should be grateful to Bishop Fadeyi for adding a book like this to our shelves. It is a book for every family and a "must read" too for all those who aspire for positions of leadership.

Dr. Abiodun Alao

Conflict Security and Development Group,

King's College, University of London

Preface

This book began as a revelation God impressed upon my heart. I gladly received the divine download from the Holy Spirit and preached it over and over – each time with more relish and insight.

The Lord continually inspired me to impart men (and women) on the process of becoming a father. To many this may sound quite odd – I guess you may even be saying: "Isn't it obvious how a man becomes a father?"

The honest answer to this innocent question is that the gift of Fatherhood is often misunderstood and misrepresented in society; and even more so in the church.

God has given me grace to capture His divine revelation on fatherhood and this book will reveal to you the important process of 'The making of a Father.'

Chapter by chapter it becomes clear that fatherhood spans beyond manhood, maleness, and the ability to produce sperm.

Being the first ever Father Himself, God's heart is for mankind to embrace fatherhood in all its ramifications.

I believe there is a profound need right now in the world, and particularly the church; for an understanding of the spirit of Fatherhood. The spirit of Fatherhood is not just confined to men but also has a significant place in a woman's life.

With God's inspiration, this book details the various stages of the 'making of a father'; it will open your eyes to God's plan for transiting men especially, from just being 'male' to being made into fathers. I encourage every reader to allow the many lessons in this book to permeate and bless your hearts as you discover, embark upon or even re-visit Fatherhood.

Acknowledgements

I wish to express my profound love and appreciation to my wife, Joyce and to my dear children, Elizabeth, Samuel and Emmanuel for their constant support and encouragement.

To Sister Shola Oladipo for an excellent editorial and her passion to get this book done. Thanks for helping me utilise the printing page to reach more souls for the kingdom of God.

To all the staff at CCD Group for the quality design and excellent book production.

To the Grace Outreach congregation Worldwide, partners and friends for their support and prayers.

Contents

Introduction

One of the greatest things about God the Creator are His creations. Yes - they are truly amazing, we are daily exposed to the wonders of His hand; spanning from the smallest creeping arthropod to the amazing almost theatrical dimensions of the rhinoceros! Notwithstanding, the greatest of all creations by far is that of mankind. The Bible account in **Genesis 1:26-28** is truly marvellous:

> *Then God said, "Let us make man in our image, after our likeness; and let them have dominion over the fish of the sea, and over the birds of the air, and over the cattle, and over all the earth, and over every creeping thing that creeps upon the earth." So God created man in His own image, in the image of God He created him; male and female He created them. And God blessed them, and God said to them, "Be fruitful and multiply, and fill the earth and subdue it; and have dominion over the fish of the sea and over the birds of the air and over every living thing that moves upon the earth."*

This passage clarifies three truths:

• God created mankind (us)

• God created mankind (us) in His image;

• God created mankind (us) male and female.

Being male and female are 'umbrella' categories for the two sexes, beyond that I believe God had an even more highly specialised, defined plan for male and female. He saw a further dimension, His vision spanned beyond the two 'genders'; as He made man in His own image and likeness.

It goes without saying of course, that the term 'man' in this context encapsulates both he who is 'wombless' and she who is 'woman.'

The human race is nothing less than awesome. We purvey God's handiwork in all shapes, sizes and textures, colours and creeds. Indeed, we are authentically certified as 'fearfully and wonderfully made' by God in the book of **Psalms 139:14:**

I praise you because I am fearfully and wonderfully made; your works are wonderful, I know that full well.

Research studies from the US show that the world population i.e the total population of humans on the planet Earth, is currently estimated to be 6.91 billion. (1) Imagine, in this vast multiplicity of humans each one of us has a unique purpose in life! Knowing and fulfilling these individual, tailor-made mandates for our lives puts the world in a comfortable, purposeful equilibrium beautifully in synchronisation with God Himself. Sadly, this idyllic picture is far from what we see today. Here are some quite differing statistics affecting mankind in the 21st century:

• Life expectancy of males as a global cumulative is 68.9 years – not bad, however this is alarmingly lower in the developing world where it is slashed to 47 years in Angola. (2)

• Divorce rates are creeping up all over the world leaving men, women and children's lives in tatters.

• The rates of crimes leading to death have also escalated over the last decade; in particular we see an attack on the male gender.

• The numbers of men in prisons in the United Kingdom is at its highest as are the figures for absent fathers and broken homes.

Amidst these rather perturbing facts, the truth of God will always prevail for His children! Paramount in God's will is that we live purposefully. We must fulfill what He designed us for.

Fatherhood is a purposefully awesome, yet misunderstood office. Only God makes men into fathers – not society, schooling, military or even counsellors.

Fathers are made by God; fathers are leaders, achievers, servants and champions. Fathers are part of His design to influence this dying world and set things straight.

The making of a father is a defined, carefully calculated process. It involves various stages which manifest as life experiences – mankind cannot live in God's image without the making of fathers.

Chapter 1:

The Process

There are key phases or stages in the making of a premium product. Often each stage is uniquely characterised by carefully defined processes or operating procedures. The time allocation and distinct duration between each phase is quite unique to the product. The completion of each stage is crucial to the overall successful conclusion and authenticity of the 'making' process.

Stages or processes can be likened to the steps in a recipe for making a food. Let's consider bread making for a moment. Within this staple food there are several types or varieties – white bread, brown bread, whole meal bread, Ciabatta, Pitta, Focaccia, Croissant, Naan etc…, the list goes on!

Fathers are made – it's important to understand and undergo each phase of God's making

Now contemplate that each bread type has its own distinct features which are directly related to the 'making' process. From the amounts of flour, sugar and salt; to the kneading and proving stages of the dough – the process for all of the aforementioned bread types differs. The milling or stripping of the wheat which constitutes the foundation of the bread clearly differs depending on the loaf. A wholemeal loaf for instance needs more kneading and proving than pitta bread which is somewhat flatter and void of yeast. It is fair to conclude that the secret to the authenticity of

Society daily fumbles woefully in its attempt to make fathers

a product is centered on the successful completion of the stages within the 'making' process. This, combined with the skill of the manufacturer is what gives a product it uniqueness, functionality and longevity, and in the case of bread its delicious taste too!

Fathers are made

The process of making a father is one of the most important processes God accomplishes in a man. The progression and timing of God's making of fathers is defined and directed by God the master builder and moulder. God uses situations and circumstances, plus the element of timing, to take man on a life-changing excursion where the final destination is Fatherhood. Fathers are made – a father is the end product of the 'making' process. It's important to understand and undergo each phase of God's making so that the end product will meet its prescribed purpose.

Have you ever noticed how particular we can be when purchasing a product? We often examine who made the product and judge the product's quality on the country of manufacture e.g. made in US versus made in China!

Basically we can safely conclude that wherever and whoever

makes the product is pivotal to its quality.

Note that not all fathers are made by God. We see society daily fumbling woefully in its attempt to make fathers – the fall out rate and casualties are enormous. There are many systems trying to 'make' fathers.

Isaiah 9:6 illustrates the phases in making of a father in the life of Jesus:

> *For to us a child is born, to us a son is given, and the government will be on his shoulders. And he will be called Wonderful Counselor, Mighty God, Everlasting Father, Prince of Peace.*

From the passage we see a **child** is born, from this he becomes a **son** who is given, this son becomes a **father**, in this case - the everlasting Father. We see Jesus Christ going through these stages. Note that Jesus was **not** born as an everlasting Father, rather he underwent process.

A child is born,
a son is given,
a father is made

Once born, a baby begins life as being essentially male or female. Even whilst in the womb, curious parents can (and often do) inquire of their baby's sex. Modern technology and a skilled radiographer are commonplace in most antenatal units. The ultrasound scan tells the expectant parents whether their baby is male or female. At this point, notice that the parents are *not* concerned about whether the child is a father or not. The male has to become a man, just as the female needs to become a woman.

It is possible for a male to age without becoming a man, he simply moves from being a young male to an old male. Old males are not real men, never living as real men.

A male can age without becoming a man... there are many males but very few fathers

To be become a real man, a male needs to understand that God's purposes must permeate his entire life so that they can overflow into the lives of others. Being a real man is not always age dependant, it's amazing to see that many young males are in fact living like real men, their reasoning and interactions are remarkably in tune with God Himself. This can be solely attributed to the grace of God that comes upon a man or woman's life and causes you to live beyond your natural age in terms of wisdom, attitude and personality. Friend, it is not about age it is about grace! God's immeasurable grace causes His own to stand out in all situations.

I recall several moments where men and women have apprehended me and remarked on the way in which I have conducted my life as a young man. I humbly attribute this to the amazing grace of God; He clearly endowed me with what my late father respected and called 'a young man clothed in the garments of an elder.' For this I am truly grateful.

God makes fathers out of real men

Even Abraham, like his younger descendant Joseph, who was his great-great-great grandson, went through a process of making. Let's review **Genesis 17: 1-5**:

> [1] When Abram was ninety-nine years old, the LORD appeared to him and said, "I am God Almighty; walk before me faithfully and be blameless. [2] Then I will make my covenant between me and you

and will greatly increase your numbers." [3] Abram fell facedown, and God said to him, [4] "As for me, this is my covenant with you: You will be the father of many nations. [5] No longer will you be called Abram; your name will be Abraham, for I have made you a father of many nations

Let us observe the process which Abraham underwent; he 'transited' from *'thou shall be'* to *'I have made you.'* This transition is commemorated with the name change of Abram. He went from being an 'exalted father' to a father of 'many nations!'

The world lacks fathers made by God

It is paramount that we are aware of the transition periods in our own lives. In the world today, there are many males but very few fathers. The greatest challenges facing nations in a world filled with crimes and lawlessness is the lack of fathers who have been made by God. The United States of America is based on the principles and legacy of their 'founding fathers' all of whom had a godly heritage. Conversely, many nations struggle to identify fathers made by God. Fathers will be those that will either 'build up' – made by God or those made by the devil, that destroy.

The next three chapters will take you on a detailed tour of the phases or stages that comprise the making of a father.

I will use the life of Joseph as a 'case study' to help illustrate each of these unique steps towards fatherhood.

Chapter 2:

Phase One - Stripping

The life of Joseph carefully illustrates the phases or processes involved in the making of a father. His interesting and often troublesome transition from the comfort of his home to the pit, prison and palace frame an extremely important part of him ultimately becoming a father.

Let's begin our review of Joseph's life in **Genesis 45:1-13.**

> [1] *Then Joseph could no longer control himself before all his attendants, and he cried out, "Have everyone leave my presence!" So there was no one with Joseph when he made himself known to his brothers.* [2] *And he wept so loudly that the Egyptians heard him, and Pharaoh's household heard about it.*
>
> [3] *Joseph said to his brothers, "I am Joseph! Is my father still living?" But his brothers were not able to answer him, because they were terrified at his presence.*
>
> [4] *Then Joseph said to his brothers, "Come close to me." When they had done so, he said, "I am your brother Joseph, the one you sold into Egypt!* [5] *And now, do not be distressed and do not be angry with yourselves for selling me here, because it was to save lives that God sent me ahead of you.* [6] *For two years now there has been famine in the land and for the next five years there will be no ploughing and reaping.* [7] *But God sent me ahead of you to preserve for you a remnant on earth and to save your lives by a great deliverance.*
>
> [8] *"So then, it was not you who sent me here, but God. He made me*

father to Pharaoh, lord of his entire household and ruler of all Egypt.
⁹ Now hurry back to my father and say to him, 'this is what your son
Joseph says: God has made me lord of all Egypt. Come down to
me; don't delay. ¹⁰ You shall live in the region of Goshen and be near
me—you, your children and grandchildren, your flocks and herds,
and all you have. ¹¹ I will provide for you there, because five years of
famine are still to come. Otherwise you and your household and all
who belong to you will become destitute.'

¹² "You can see for yourselves, and so can my brother Benjamin,
that it is really I who am speaking to you. ¹³ Tell my father about all
the honour accorded me in Egypt and about everything you have
seen. And bring my father down here quickly."

In verse 8 we see that Joseph states *'God has made me a father to Pharaoh.'* The actual use of the word 'made' in this text is interesting. Joseph attributes his 'making' to God; he is submitting to his brethren that God is the manufacturer of his fatherhood.

Joseph was empathic about the source of his making – he made it known that God had made him a father to Pharaoh. Indeed we can speculate here that Pharaoh is likely to have been old

Refining involves the alteration of raw materials before they become the final product

enough to actually father Joseph - nevertheless God made Joseph a father to Pharaoh. Envisage this: Pharaoh was a title given to Egyptian rulers, the title or office was accompanied by an infamous personality for being a terror and menace to all around.

Pharaohs were known to terrorise communities. It is this very same terror that God caused Joseph to become a father over! Joseph was the father over an entity that was a threat to the lives of many. I pray that God will cause you to be father over those things that have terrorised you.

Joseph being made a father over Pharaoh was the end result of a process that he underwent. The actual process can be split into differing stages. The first of these stages is stripping.

Stripping: the first and vital part

In the manufacturing industry it is often necessary to alter the state of the raw materials before they become the final product. This is often known as refining. In food technology (which I have studied extensively) the principle of refining is very apparent; the raw materials often need to be stripped, peeled, scraped or broken down. In many cases, the actual potency of an ingredient is not released until it is stripped. Take for instance a clove of garlic. In order to make use of the clove, you first need to remove it from the bulb. This involves some level of stripping. Once the clove is separated it then needs to be peeled or stripped and chopped. The several outer layers of the garlic are no good for cooking our delicious foods; and to be honest, unless removed, those outer layers mask the release of the garlic's flavoursome potential.

Joseph needed to be stripped before he became a father. His outer layer was one of pride. According to the Oxford online dictionary (3), pride is defined as a 'feeling of deep pleasure or satisfaction derived from achievements, qualities, or possessions that do one credit.'

There were definitely such elements present in the life of Joseph – they needed to go.

Joseph, like any other child was born and as a son he was given. However, for Joseph to move on to manhood and fatherhood,

God had to refine him. He needed to undergo all that befell him in
Genesis 37:12-24:

> [12] Now his brothers had gone to graze their father's flocks near
> Shechem, [13] and Israel said to Joseph, "As you know, your brothers
> are grazing the flocks near Shechem. Come, I am going to send
> you to them." "Very well," he replied. [14] So he said to him, "Go and
> see if all is well with your brothers and with the flocks, and bring
> word back to me." Then he sent him off from the Valley of Hebron.
> When Joseph arrived at Shechem, [15] a man found him wandering
> around in the fields and asked him, "What are you looking for?" [16]
> He replied, "I'm looking for my brothers. Can you tell me where they
> are grazing their flocks?" [17] "They have moved on from here," the
> man answered. "I heard them say, 'Let's go to Dothan.'" So Joseph
> went after his brothers and found them near Dothan. [18] But they saw
> him in the distance, and before he reached them, they plotted to kill
> him. [19] "Here comes that dreamer!" they said to each other. [20] "Come
> now, let's kill him and throw him into one of these cisterns and say
> that a ferocious animal devoured him. Then we'll see what comes
> of his dreams." [21] When Reuben heard this, he tried to rescue him
> from their hands. "Let's not take his life," he said. [22] "Don't shed any
> blood. Throw him into this cistern here in the desert, but don't lay a
> hand on him." Reuben said this to rescue him from them and take
> him back to his father. [23] So when Joseph came to his brothers,
> they stripped him of his robe—the richly ornamented robe he was
> wearing— [24] and they took him and threw him into the cistern. Now
> the cistern was empty; there was no water in it.

Stripped of Pride

Joseph was guilty of pride - it is likely that the origin of his pride
was from the fact that his parents displayed a very special love for
him. The Bible makes us understand that Joseph was the much
'longed for' son born to Jacob (Israel) and his sweetheart Rachel.
His father loved him with an especially great magnitude – this he
openly displayed by providing for him a coat of many colours.
None of Joseph's brothers had been bestowed with such an
honour.

Bible historians have pointed out that the 'coat' was probably a long 'tunic like' garment of heavy luxurious cloth, often darned with dignitaries in mind. Joseph loved to wear his very opulent coat of many colours.

It is important to appreciate that God permitted Joseph's brothers to strip him of the coat of many colours. As we see from the Bible account in **Genesis 37,** it was the day that Joseph responded to his father's request, which was to go and check on his brothers as they laboured in the fields and tended their father's herds.

It seemed natural, to Joseph at least, to wear his luxurious tunic for this task so he wore his coat on that day. This does however raise the question – why on earth would Joseph wear his coat to the fields where his brothers were labouring if not to 'show-off?' Why wear the coat to check on his brothers? Did he want to remind them of how special he was? This action compounded with his ambitious dreams, annoyed his brothers.

Joseph needed to be stripped before he became a father. His outer layer was one of pride

David's stripping – a necessity from God

David is another good example of a man in the Bible who was stripped. David too was stripped of pride. The Bible points out just how David was maltreated by Saul in his fits of jealousy and malice against him. (See David's encounters in the book of **1Samuel**) All that David suffered at the hand of Saul was permitted; it was allowed in order to strip him of any pride. God had big plans for David and in order for David to succeed in being the 'planned' end product; David underwent a process which included being stripped.

Are you being stripped right now? Are you going through some 'stuff' right now? Are you praying or wishing the stripping away? Please be aware that until you are put through fire, you will not know the impurities which reside within.

Those destined for greatness must be stripped, purified, pruned, peeled and sanded down. Basically, you never know what is inside of a person until a little pressure is applied.

To be honest, David's case was a major stripping. Saul who once favoured him suddenly became his arch enemy. David was given

What David suffered at the hand of Saul was permitted; it was allowed in order to strip him of any pride

the opportunity to kill Saul on more than one occasion but knew better then to touch the Lord's anointed. Even if the anointing had departed from Saul, David dare not disrespect Saul, right up until the end, David addressed Saul as 'father.' David decided that he would not sin against God. The stripping was painful and uncomfortable but was necessary – it served to yield great results in David's life.

It's interesting to hear people say that they need the help of God to be successful or to 'make it' in life.

If ever there was a time that we need God it is when we have made it. We need him more when we are successful than when we were in need; we need Him more in our riches than our poverty! There is much more to life than 'the anointing to make it'; once we have 'made it' we must remain focused. It is not just about breakthrough – indeed much of what we call breakthrough, for many has resulted in breakdown. I pray that you remain focused, in Jesus' Name!

Everyone is subject to pride; it is resident on the inside of every one of us. It lurks and waits to raise its ugly head in our lives. Do you want to be certain that it will not ruin your life as a father? Be rest assured that God will enroll you in a time of stripping as you are being made into a father. As uncomfortable as it sounds, it is an inevitable stage of the making process on the road to fatherhood.

Chapter 3:

Phase Two - The Moulding

The second phase in the overall process of making fathers is that of moulding. The term moulding is immediately suggestive of a pair of hands employed in skillfully manipulating a mound of clay. The clay undergoes a period of purposeful fashioning and crafting according to the desires of the creator or designer.

In the making of a father, this stage or phase involves the now 'pride stripped' man being moulded by the awesome hands of God, the Creator and shaper of our lives. To be precise, God carefully moulds the man into a servant. God performs this moulding by permitting various events to happen in the life of a man. These occurrences serve to initiate the moulding of the man into the 'shape' of a servant; this phase of servanthood cannot be overlooked in the making of a father.

Moulded for Servanthood

Those that become fathers are moulded and shaped into servants.

To the natural ear the word 'servant' often gives an impression of:

- An underling;
- Inferiority;
- Low class;
- Second best
- Or even the bottom of the pile!

This, of course, is not the case at all. For those attuned with spiritual ears, servanthood connotes greatness. That is, the true mark of greatness is servanthood.

True leaders are servant leaders – they live to serve others.

One of my greatest personal prayers is that the Lord will never let me lose sight of being a servant. Friend, please imprint this on the forefront of your mind: being ever reminded that **true leaders are servants.**

It is sad to observe that in many cultures (not excluding my own West African heritage) the concept of servanthood in leadership is somewhat strange. In many cases it is deemed appropriate to be bossy and overbearing when occupying a position of leadership.

The clay undergoes a period of purposeful fashioning and crafting according to the desires of the creator or designer

Leaders in such cultures often revel in being dictatorial, inconsiderate and self centered, with little inclination to ever serve the people; but rather to be served by them. This leadership style is regrettably part and parcel of many leaders around the globe; many nations are ruined by such tyrannical forces. The church also has her fair share of such leaders – this is pitiful and desperately needs to be addressed.

Jesus – the servant leader

Contrary to man's viewpoint, Jesus our Lord came as a servant;

His mandate was to serve. Not only did this irritate the Pharisees and Sadducees, but the Jewish people themselves also found Jesus' actions atypical of a leader as they had expected. Please be reminded that the Jews expected a somewhat more grandiose entry of their Messiah.

Jesus' preaching, teaching and daily display of servanthood caused the very people He came to serve, to actually reject Him.

The Bible records this in the book of John:

He came unto his own, and his own received him not. (John 1:11)

Sometimes people today equate serving to weakness, oh, how acutely wrong such assumptions are!

Joseph moulded into a servant

How did this happen?

Well, if we revisit the original text outlining our case study of Joseph's life, we see in **Genesis 37**, that God allowed Joseph to be sold to the Ishmaelites:

Genesis 37:26-28

26 Judah said to his brothers, "What will we gain if we kill our brother and cover up his blood? 27 Come, let's sell him to the Ishmaelites and not lay our hands on him; after all, he is our brother, our own flesh and blood." His brothers agreed. 28 So when the Midianite merchants came by, his brothers pulled Joseph up out of the cistern and sold him for twenty shekels[a] of silver to the Ishmaelites, who took him to Egypt

Suddenly the 'golden boy' is sold as a common slave and taken to Egypt. With the loss of his marvellous coat of many colours (stripping), Joseph undergoes a somewhat painful - but necessary, moulding process.

In verse 36 of **Genesis chapter 37**, we actually see that Joseph was sold again as part of a transaction between the Midianites and one of Pharaoh's officials in Egypt. This was how Joseph ended up in the house of Potiphar – the captain of the guard.

...And the Midianites sold him into Egypt unto Potiphar, an officer of Pharaoh's, and captain of the guard.

Take a moment and imagine Joseph's thoughts as his habitual stability and joyous life of being papa Jacob's favourite is overturned. Here we see Joseph, who was formerly used to being the centre of attention in the confines of his father's house; in the 'office' of servanthood in the house of a foreigner. It's likely that as daddy's 'favourite boy', young brother Joseph was used to being served and perhaps even having people responsible for his laundry, meal preparation and other domestic chores. And now in Potiphar's house see how the tables had turned! Joseph is now a servant, an errand boy with no special status. I think it would not be unfair to call him a houseboy.

But what did all this represent? The answer is clear: it was a character moulding and building process for him. He was being

For those attuned with spiritual ears, servanthood connotes greatness

shaped into a servant, no longer being served by mum, dad or his many brothers and sisters. Joseph was now the servant.

I suspect that many of you reading this book could be at a juncture in life which corresponds to God's process of moulding you. Are you in a work place where it seems as if you are treated like a servant? Well, it may be that God is testing you. Please be aware,

God doesn't tempt, but God will test you. Perhaps, you are in a local church where you are enduring a rather uncomfortable 'moulding' process? Beloved, be glad when called upon for the so called 'menial' roles; you are in the making process – let God mould you into servanthood – for where He is taking you is truly great!

Let's take a closer look at servanthood, as this is the key to the shaping of a father's life.

Here are some thought provoking quotes on servanthood and servant leaders

> *"Leaders we admire do not place themselves at the centre; they place others there. They do not seek the attention of people; they give it to others. They do not focus on satisfying their own aims and desires; they look for ways to respond to the needs and interests of their constituents. They are not self-centred; they concentrate on the constituent. . . Leaders serve a purpose and the people who have made it possible for them to lead . . . . In serving a purpose, leaders strengthen credibility by demonstrating that they are not in it for themselves; instead, they have the interests of the institution, department, or team and its constituents at heart. Being a servant may not be what many leaders had in mind when they choose to take responsibility for the vision and direction of their organization or team, but serving others is the most glorious and rewarding of all leadership tasks."* ~ **James Kouzes and Barry Posner in "Credibility: How Leaders Gain and Lose It, Why People Demand It".**

> *"People do not care how much you know until they know how much you care."* ~ **John C. Maxwell**

> *"Being a leader who serves is very different from being a servant leader."* ~ **Isabel O. Lopez**

> *"Servant-leadership is more than a concept, it is a fact. Any great leader, by which I also mean an ethical leader of any group, will see herself or himself as a servant of that group and will act accordingly."* ~ **M. Scott Peck**

> *"A person who is worthy of being a leader wants power not for*

himself, but in order to be of service." ~ **US Senator Sam J. Ervin, Jr.**

"Use power to help people. For we are given power not to advance our own purposes or to make a great show in the world, not a name. There is but one just use of power and it is to serve people." ~ **US President George Bush**

"The measure of a leader is not the number of people who serve the leader, but the number of people served by the leader." ~ **Adapted from a quote by John C. Maxwell.**

"Whatever our career may be, true leadership means to receive power from God and to use it under Gods rule to serve people in God's way." ~ **Leighton Ford**

"A Godly Leader finds strength by realizing his weakness, finds authority by being under authority, finds direction by laying down his own plans, finds vision by seeing the needs of others, finds credibility by being an example, finds loyalty by expressing compassion, finds honour by being faithful, finds greatness by being a servant." ~ **Roy Lessin**

"Servant-leadership is more than a concept, it is a fact. Any great leader, by which I also mean an ethical leader of any group, will see herself or himself as a servant of that group and will act accordingly." ~ **M. Scott Peck**

"As you wait upon the Lord, you learn to see things from His perspective, move at His pace, and function under His directives. Waiting times are growing times and learning times. As you quiet your heart, you enter His peace: as you sense your weakness, you receive His strength: as you lay down your will, you hear His calling. When you mount up, you are being lifted by the wind of His Spirit . . . When you move ahead; you are sensitive to His timing. When you act, you give as yourself only to the things He has asked you to do." ~ **Roy Lessin**

"Everybody can be great because anybody can serve. You don't have to have a college degree to serve. You don't have to make your subject and verb agree to serve. You only need a heart full of grace. A soul generated by love." ~ **Martin Luther King Jr. as quoted in Even Eagles Need a Push p. 109.**

Graham Kendrick, one of the most prolifically blessed song composers of Christian worship songs; penned a moving song about Jesus. In the words note the title: The servant King. It is based on **Philippians 2:4-8; Matthew 26:39; Isaiah 53:7 and Ephesians 6:7.**

The lyrics go thus:

From heaven You came, helpless Babe, Entered our world, Your glory veiled; Not to be served, but to serve, And give Your life that we might live. This is our God, the Servant King; He calls us now to follow Him; to bring our lives as a daily offering of worship to the Servant King.

There in the garden of tears, my heavy load He chose to bear; His heart with sorrow was torn, "Yet not my will, but Yours," He said. Come, see His hands and His feet, The scars that speak of sacrifice, Hands that flung stars into space, To cruel nails surrendered. So let us learn how to serve, and in our lives enthrone Him; Each other's needs to prefer, for it is Christ we're serving

The moulding phase is indeed an essential part of the making of a father. I pray God's strengthens and enlightens you as you prepare to experience this phase.s

"People do not care how much you know until they know how much you care."

~ John C. Maxwell

Chapter 4:

Phase Three
Sharpened for Fatherhood

As we keenly follow the life of Joseph, let me introduce you to yet another phase towards his ultimate destination of becoming a father. So far, we have covered two processes in the making a father - **stripping** and **moulding** into servanthood. Joseph's next

The blade of a knife is the pinnacle of its functionality or usefulness and the knife remains unhelpful if it is not sharpened.

stop on this magnanimous journey of life leads him to becoming spiritually '**sharpened**' for fatherhood.

This part of the progression is even more acute and precise than the preceding ones. To introduce this, permit me to direct your mind to the aspect of sharpening.

The danger of being blunt

The picture I wish to paint is that of a cutting implement - let's say a knife. The blade of a knife is made from various raw materials – usually stainless steel. The steel itself is sourced from its raw state, then moulded and shaped for its function – for example the blade of a dining knife is shaped differently to a butcher's knife because their functions are very different. The blade of a knife is the pinnacle of its functionality or usefulness and the knife remains unhelpful if it is not sharpened.

Imagine using a blunt knife to cut a piece of steak. It will eventually do the job, but I suspect it will take longer, require more effort, and be quite messy; and indeed leave the diner (the person eating the meal) in a less than satisfactory state. Have you noticed that unsharpened implements often leave a jagged, uneven edge? The untidy edges reveal gaps and lack of precision to the finished product.

God sharpens fathers by filing down, sanding away and excavating all excesses that hinder spiritual acuity

A surgeon's knife is unmistakably useless and indeed dangerous if it is not sharpened; a critical surgical operation is jeopardised by blunt instruments. Can you now see how important the issue of sharpening can be?

This phase of sharpening in the making if a father is inimitable. A father **must** be sharp and sound in his spirit. God sharpens fathers by filing down, sanding away and excavating all excesses that hinder spiritual acuity.

How many times have you been in a room with a man who lacked that soundness, acuteness or sharpness in the Word? God's expectation of fathers is that they are not blunt, not impotent and requiring extra effort. This is why, in the making of a father – sharpening must take place.

Whilst being sharpened, much debris is lost in the unneeded filings. The excess or dross is keenly cut away in an often painful process.

Shaving away pride

Joseph's period of sharpening is synonymous with 'tough times' in his life. Take note of this for your own life, sharpening often looks like a trial from the devil, but please know it may be that God is dealing with you, especially in the area of pride. Perhaps Joseph was thinking he had 'arrived' at his place of comfort as Potiphar's servant – God had in place a plan to ensure he was 'sharpened.' In **Genesis chapter 39** in the early verses, we see that he was favoured:

4 Joseph found favour in his eyes and became his attendant. Potiphar put him in charge of his household and he entrusted to his care everything he owned.

5 From the time he put him in charge of his household and of all that he owned, the LORD blessed the household of the Egyptian because of Joseph. The blessing of the LORD was on everything Potiphar had, both in the house and in the field.

6 So he left in Joseph's care everything he had; with Joseph in charge, he did not concern himself with anything except the food he ate. Now Joseph was well-built and handsome,

Genesis 39: 4-6

From verse 7 onwards, things took a different shape, he was lied against by the madam of the house following her request that he 'lie with her.' Here I purport that contrary to popular allusions, it was not exclusively Potiphar's wife that was the 'issue.' Joseph

proved to have an issue with pride too. Notice how he responds
to her:

> *But he refused. With me in charge, he told her, my master does not
> concern himself with anything in the house; everything he owns he
> has entrusted to my care.*
>
> *[9] No-one is greater in this house than I am. My master has withheld
> nothing from me except you, because you are his wife. How then
> could I do such a wicked thing and sin against God?*
>
> *[10] And though she spoke to Joseph day after day, he refused to go
> to bed with her or even to be with her.*
>
> **Genesis 39:8-10**

He displayed an air of self confidence as he addressed Mrs.
Potiphar. He was not slow in telling her that there is 'none greater
than I in this household!' He went on to substantiate his response
asking 'How can I, do this great wickedness?' It seems apparent
that there was a lot of 'I' going on and less of God!

Dreamer becomes Interpreter

In verse 20, Joseph went from being a palace servant to a
prisoner - hard times indeed! In actual fact he matured from
being a dreamer to becoming an interpreter. Basically, he needed
to be sharpened – and prison was the place that God had chosen
for him.

In chapter 40, Joseph meets the butler and baker, both of whom
dreamt a dream each which needed an interpreter.

A complete man

Note how Joseph puts aside his own agenda and is ready to help
others. In fact he goes to the trouble of asking them why they
were sad, he still had time to notice others in trouble in the midst
of his own trouble.

[6] When Joseph came to them the next morning, he saw that they were dejected.

[7] So he asked Pharaoh's officials who were in custody with him in his master's house, why are your faces so sad today?

Genesis 40:6-7

Joseph was complete and secure in himself and offered help in interpreting the dreams. Notice how he now attributes interpretations to God first, in comparison to the 'I 'statements in Potiphar's house:

…. 'Do not interpretations belong to God?'

Genesis 40:8

Joseph, though being sharpened felt no need to compete with his fellow prisoners in having their needs met before his. Remember he was going through his own problems; he could have refused to acknowledge or help with theirs.

Isn't it true that when we are going through our low moments it's the most unlikely time for us to lend a helping hand? We are so deeply drowned and wallowing in our own 'stuff' that we ignore others around us who are in need – such behaviour is a sign of

As real men it is important to know that the expanse of the sky is such that no two birds ever collide.

immaturity. Joseph was able to put his dreams aside and became an interpreter; even though his dreams remained un-interpreted.

It takes a mature a man to put his dreams aside for another. The height of insecurity is manifested when a man is so threatened by another's success that he will stoop as low as to withhold information that helps his fellow man. Such men as husbands are often even threatened by the success of their wives – they are often quick to hold them back in business and even in ministry. As real men, it is important to know that the expanse of the sky is such that no two birds ever collide. In other words, there is plenty of room to accommodate your successes, your wife's success and that of your fellow man.

If that insecure man is you, allow God to sharpen you – you need to be a real man and a real father; your behaviour shows that you have not 'arrived.' I pray and believe that even as you read this book, your change begins today!

Ready for Fatherhood

Joseph performed this act of kindness, and in turn asked that the butler remember him – of course this did not happen and Joseph remained in prison for some years. One day Pharaoh had a dream which needed interpretation – no one could help, then Joseph was remembered!

Joseph was summoned and interpreted the dream accurately and Pharaoh was so thankful that he instated Joseph to oversee his house and rule the people according to his word.

We now see the 'father making' process that led Joseph to his discourse with his brothers in **Genesis 45**

> *"So then, it was not you who sent me here, but God. He made me father to Pharaoh, lord of his entire household and ruler of all Egypt."*
>
> *Genesis 45:8*

The sharpening of Joseph prepared him for what was next – becoming a father. He was made a father by God – by virtue of the processes he had been through from the stripping, moulding and sharpening we see Joseph move from a child – son – man

– mature man – father. I am sure you will agree that this stage of sharpening was worth every bit of the journey. This final 'pruning' set Joseph up for where he was destined to be.

Your destiny is certain when you allow God to 'make' you, it will not be easy, comfy or even fun but it will be worth it.

Chapter 5:

Final Phase - Divinely Furnished

The overall process of Joseph's 'making' led to the triumphant result: Joseph was made a 'father' by God as well as being honoured and favoured by Pharaoh.

Joseph became a signet carrier – he became an edict maker, a sealant to laws and decrees

So Pharaoh asked them, "Can we find anyone like this man, one in whom is the spirit of God?"

Genesis 41:38

Pharaoh took his ring off and put it on Joseph, a sign of total confidence and reverence to the anointing he carried. Joseph became a signet carrier – he became an edict maker, a sealant to laws and decrees. Open access to the treasury of Egypt was his – a powerful position of trust and prestige.

This is so significant: the awarding of a gold ring and chain for the same person who had his coat of many colours taken from him. Friend, there are times in life when what we struggle for is sometimes so infinitesimal, so microscopically minuscule in comparison to God's plan for us. The coat that he treasured and struggled to hold on to bore little resemblance to the adornment placed upon him as 'father to pharaoh.'

Many men (and women) grapple with something, seeking to keep hold of it – a habit, a mindset perhaps, or even what they deem as success. Some of what you see as treasures or achievements needs to be relinquished to God. He will strip them away, mould and sharpen you into fatherhood, and give you true honour and grace. Such divine embellishment is in store for those who endure the 'test' or process of the making of a father. What God has in store is greater than what you are holding onto right now.

Divine embellishment is in store for those who endure the 'test' or process of the making of a father

The loss of the coat of many colours was nothing compared to the gain, prestige, honour and blessing bestowed on Joseph by Pharaoh. Joseph was **divinely furnished**.

I have spent the major part of this book revealing to you the phases and processes of becoming a father. The good news is that it does not end here at divine furnishing. God is progressive, never static – there is no end to His glory. Your fatherhood journey is one where you continually move from glory to glory. Whilst encased in this flesh we must be daily stripped – pride has a way of creeping up on even the 'best' of fathers, For this reason we regularly undergo the process of making – in actual fact it is never as extreme and intense as the first process but is definitely ongoing.

Like the apostle Paul we must 'die daily' to self....this becomes more and more of a reality when we are stripped, moulded and sharpened by the awesome hand of God. John the Baptist also noted this as he spoke of Christ:

"You must increase and I must decrease" **John 3:30**

As fathers, we need to daily decrease so that God can increase in us.

Your responsibility to Fathers

It is truly a blessing to have 'fathers in our lives, they are a gift from God. Both biological and spiritual fathers have served to shape individuals, families, communities and nations. The influence of a godly father lives on as a testament of God's divine hand guiding, encouraging, rebuking and comforting the children God has placed under his jurisdiction. When God brings a father-figure into your life, you have responsibilities – let me expand on a few of these:

Recognition

You must recognise them – a dictionary definition of such recognition is: to know, to be aware, to identify and acknowledge; to accept, to notice and show appreciation.

In the book of **Matthew chapter 16**, Jesus engaged His disciples with a somewhat profound conversation. They were the same people that had been with Him for a while, and He said to them, *"Who do the people say I am?"* I can imagine some of them scratching their heads, hesitantly processing their answers. They responded with various statements, including the report that

"Some say you are Elijah." Jesus went further and said to them *"but you my disciples, who do you, say I am?"* This time only the disciple Peter by the Spirit spoke up and said, *"You are The Christ the Son of the living God."* Jesus then said to Peter, *"Flesh and blood did not reveal that to you."* It took God to help Peter to recognise who Christ was. Christ was not just the Saviour amongst them, He was a Father to them, and nevertheless, they did not recognise Him. Some of the disciples based their recognition on what the other people had said.

Later on in **Matthew Chapter 17, verses 1-8**, He took three disciples to the mountain of transfiguration. Now on this mountain Jesus was transfigured before them and they recognised the Christ.

> *And after six days Jesus took Peter, James, and John his brother, and lead them up into an high mountain by themselves, And He was transfigured before them: and his face did shine as the sun, and his clothes became as white as the light. And, behold, there appeared unto them Moses and Elijah talking with him. Then answered Peter, and said unto Jesus, Lord, it is good for us to be here: if thou wish let us make here three tabernacles; one for you, and one for Moses, and one for Elijah. (Peter was just hysterical.) While he was still speaking, behold, a bright cloud overshadowed them: and suddenly a voice out of the cloud, which said, "this is my beloved Son, in whom I am well pleased; hear him." And when the disciples heard it, they fell on their face, and were greatly afraid. And Jesus came and touched them, and said, Arise, and be not afraid. And when they had lifted up their eyes, they saw no man, Jesus only.*

May God help us to recognise the fathers He has brought into our lives. Jesus had to take them up to the mountain to recognise who He was. How often do we fail to recognise those God brings into our lives? How can it be that a natural or spiritual father is divinely placed so close to us, but we do not recognise them?

In some ways natural fathers have a way of enforcing recognition, and it is less likely that they are mistaken for someone else, however caution is needed to ensure that we do not miss the 'spiritual blessings' available to us via our biological fathers. How often have you said of your natural father 'it's just daddy talking again?' When in fact you have taken for granted that your natural father has been given deep spiritual embodiment specifically for your growth and advancement – I say, be careful how you belittle your father and his counsel.

In the spiritual realm, God must be allowed to do the asserting of recognition, but still the people also have to be willing to want to know. It takes God Himself to open the eyes of His people to see their spiritual fathers for who they are. Many have sadly viewed

When God brings a father figure into your life, you have responsibilities towards them

age, position, articulation and even nationality as signs of who their spiritual fathers are! Oh how sadly limited we are in the flesh! Your spiritual father is not necessarily older than you. Fatherhood is not about age, but it's about grace. To God's glory I continue to father many who are several years, even decades older than me - this is divine and not natural at all; God's gift of fatherhood extends beyond that. An old man is not automatically a father; equally a young mature man is not to be despised as a father. Be wise – discern well, recognise the father figure He has brought into your life.

Respect

To respect is to give them high regard, honour, esteem and to care for them. I believe that this is a teaching which is missing in many of our lives. To disrespect the father over you is to dishonor the God who has called him. Without sounding too hard – I must not shy away from this truth. Many have experienced difficulties and hardship due to the dishonor bestowed upon the father(s) in their lives. Be sure that it is difficult to receive anything from a source that you fail to respect.

Paul said that such are deserving of double honour:

Let the elders that rule well be counted worthy of double honour, especially they who labour in the word and doctrine.

1Tim 5:17

Samuel's sons dishonoured the counsel of their father who was both spiritual and biological head over them. They both experienced a cheerless end to their lives. Lot in his disregard for Abraham suffered loss and turmoil in his life

Timothy honoured Paul – we see this by his constant heeding to Paul whom he affectionately asserted as his father.

Even David honoured Saul whilst in enmity with him – he did not agree with the way he was being treated but still honoured Saul who was trying to kill him.

Reward

Reward is a return made for something done. The world has a way of giving awards to those who have done well. We see sports awards, film awards, literary awards, comedy awards...the list is endless!

In your place of work, at the end of the month, you receive a salary because of the labour you have put in. It's not because your face is looking good, or your attire is particularly 'sharp.' They do not give you a reward and say, "Boy you look more handsome, let's give you a salary increase." They do not care about your face; they care about your input. Your work appraisal is based on what you have done. In business, achievements are rewarded either in cash or in kind.

The Bible says in **1Tim 5:18**, *'a labourer is worthy of his reward.'*

Paul also said in **Galatians 4:19:**

> *"My little child whom I travail again until Christ be formed in them."*

It takes labour or travail to produce results. On the few occasions where opportune, I have witnessed the natural travail of a woman in childbirth, it takes pain.

Now look beyond just the natural process of the giving of birth to the raising of a child, it is costly, energy expensive and very intense.

Surely, such labour is worthy of reward!

Points to remember:

- Divine furnishing is the pinnacle in the often cyclical process of the making of fathers.

- We must not forget our duties towards our fathers.

Chapter 6:

The Spirit of Fatherhood

At the beginning of this book you may recall my statement that 'fatherhood' is not just for men...sounds odd huh? Well, being a father is more of a spiritual call and not just a 'physical' presence.

There are times when a woman can literally be playing the role of a father because fathering is not limited to the gender of a male, I am referring to those instances when in the absence of a male figure, a woman assumes the role of a father. That is why in the Bible we have people like Deborah (Judges Chapter 4) who championed the cause of God for His people.

> fathering is not limited to the gender of a male... there are times when in the absence of man, a woman assumes the role of a father

The Bible also carefully narrates the beautiful story of Ruth and Naomi which exemplifies a woman's role as a father figure in the life of Ruth. (See Ruth chapters 1-4)

After the sad death of Naomi's husband and sons, she was left with her two daughters in- law Ruth and Orpah. In her bitterness of heart, Naomi urged the two young widows to leave her and find for themselves new husbands. But Ruth zealously refused and adopted Naomi's God and people to be hers. Tenacious Ruth became the 'child' of Naomi who became the 'father figure.' Ruth recognised Naomi, she respected Naomi and she rewarded Naomi.

> *But Ruth replied, "Don't urge me to leave you or to turn back from you. Where you go I will go, and where you stay I will stay. Your people will be my people and your God my God.*
>
> **Ruth 1:16**

In the process of time, the much debased women whom all had given up on suddenly experienced God turn things around for them. At the appointed time and due to obedience to her father figure Naomi; Ruth married a husband. She gave birth to Obed

There are father figures that have made an indelibly positive mark on many lives; sadly there are also the opposite

who is part of the lineage of King David of Judah, and automatically Ruth was the great, great grandparent of King David.   Since Jesus' lineage stems from this awesome story too – being the Lion of the tribe of Judah -   you cannot look at the genealogy of Jesus without mentioning Ruth. Ruth was connected to a father figure that helped the process in the form of Naomi. That is what true father figures do; they help the process of you becoming what God has made you to be; they are to be a blessing and not a curse.

You may ask why you need to recognise, respect, and reward the father figure in your life. The reasons are:

 • So that you can fully receive what God wants to pass to you through him or her.

In the Bible, Esau and Jacob were two brothers born of the same father - Isaac. While Jacob fully received the father's blessing, Esau only received a partial blessing. In the scriptures when Isaac prayed for his sons, he also prayed a blessing for Esau, he said 'you will serve your brother,' that was a blessing too, but a far cry from a 'full' blessing. Inasmuch as I do not like eating half course meals in place of the full course, I do not like the idea of 'half' or partial blessings. You will remember that at the time that Isaac was planting that blessing, those three things were in place, they had to respect, reward and recognise their father. Issac was of course richer than his sons, and if he wanted, he could have ordered as much venison as he wished if he was hungry! He did not have to rely on his sons to do this.

Please understand that Issac was not necessarily hungry, his request was made rather to symbolise that there are things you can do to 'provoke' the blessing. True fathers are raised to bless the children. So Jacob provoked something out of his father and he received the full blessing.

 • That it may be well with you

'Honour Thy father and thy mother so that you days may be long and it may be well with you.'

Ephesians 6:12

The words 'that you may live long' are meant not just in terms of longevity or living to a ripe old age, it goes beyond that. To live long is to have a long lasting influence even after you may have slept in the Lord. There are people who only lived for 50 or 60 years, but the influence and the foot print they have left on the earth cannot be erased. Conversely, there are those that lived for 120 years and you will never even know where they were buried. May you live long and may it be well with you in the Name of Jesus.

Another example is the relationship between Esther and Mordecai. Clearly, Mordecai was not the natural father of Esther, but rather an uncle. Just like many of us in the natural, there are father figures in many uncles. It was this same Mordecai that was instrumental in the process for Esther to reach and fulfill her destiny.

You will recall that at one stage she came so close to making a mess of things and even neglecting her destiny, but thank God for this credible father figure who reminded in **Esther 4:14**

> *"For if you remain silent at this time, relief and deliverance for the Jews will arise from another place, but you and your father's family will perish. And who knows but that you have come to royal position for such a time as this?"*

> Esther 4:14

Suddenly, Esther arose and took a 'glorious risk'. You cannot talk about the history of the Jews without talking about Esther. Fathers are raised to help a process. That is how Mordecai influenced the purpose of God in her life.

Fathers should make a positive difference to our lives

There are father figures that have made an indelibly positive mark on many lives; sadly there are also the opposite. There are some of us who have come in contact with fathers that have made a negative difference in our lives. These may have been biological or spiritual father figures who have really done more harm than good. What do you do with such a father?

Some of these fathers have abandoned the real mandate for

fatherhood and trespassed their children's lives with abuse - sexually, mentally and emotionally. Many have endured such painful experiences, rather than that father being a blessing, he has abused you. Many have suffered from their father's denying or rejecting them as children and refusing to perform their fatherly role.

Even where there is no abuse or rejection, some may have suffered because of jealousy. Such was the case with David and Saul. Don't you know that Saul rejected David, all because of

> There are people who only lived for 50 or 60 years, but the influence and the foot print they have left on the earth cannot be erased

jealousy! So - what do you do with such a father, where it seems as though rather than being a positive influence, they are making a negative difference?

The answer - you must for your own sake forgive him, bring the pain to Jesus – you may benefit from a counsellor in this matter; one who can lead you back to the love of Christ. Your decision to do this will have a positive effect on your whole life. If you hold on to the pain of the past you cannot receive the blessing in your future. David had to let go to become a king, Joseph had to release his brothers and reign as a father to Pharaoh.

Receive the strength to do the same today.

Let today be the beginning of a new day in your life.

Jesus is Lord!

Happy fatherhood!

21 Day Personal Revival

The role of Fatherhood invariably requires a need for Godly transformation in our lives. Begin your transformation today as you embark on this 21 day personal revival. Use the daily prayer points and Bible passages as a guide, and be sure to keep a journal in order to record the things you feel God saying to you.

Day 1 Prayer of thanksgiving for what God has done, He's doing and He's set to do in your life. Psalm 100:1-5, Psalm 103:1-5, Psalm 136:1-26

Day 2 Prayer of dedication to do the will of God on a daily basis. Matthew 6:8-13, Romans 6:1-23, Romans 12:1-2, Luke 22:39-

Day 3 Pray for the salvation of the members of your family, friends and your nation. Psalm 2:8, Acts 16:25-34, 2Corinthians 4:3-4, Luke 15:1-31

Day 4 Pray for the restoration of backslidden and fallen members in the body of Christ. 2Corinthians 7:10, Ezekiel 18:30-32

Day 5 Ask God for the grace to live a holy life as you desire to maintain a lifestyle of sexual purity. Leviticus 20:22-26, Leviticus 19:1, Hebrews 12:14, 1Corinthians 6:18-20

Day 6   Ask God to give you an understanding heart that is filled with divine wisdom. 1Kings 3:13-18, James 1:5

Day 7   Ask God for the strength to carry out your business, ministry and family responsibilities. Psalm 27:1-14, Isaiah 40:28-31, Job 17:9

Day 8   Ask God for the grace to hear and obey His voice. John 10:4-5, Matthew 13:10-16, 1Samuel 3:1-8

Day 9   Ask God for "The Blessing." 1Chronicles 4:9-10, Genesis 12:2-3, Deuteronomy 28:1-14

Day 10   Proclaim and appropriate your victory in the blood of Jesus. Exodus 12:21-30, Revelation 12:11, 1Peter 1:17-19

Day 11   Ask God for the Spirit of boldness. Acts 4:13-31, Proverbs 28:1, 1Samuel 17:31-54

Day 12   Ask God for the wealth and riches to advance His Kingdom on earth. Psalm 112:1-10, 2Corinthians 8:9, 2Corinthians 9:8

Day 13   Ask God for the grace to walk in love. 1Corinthians 13:1-13, 1 John 2:7-11, Romans 5:1-5

Day 14   Pray for the Spirit of unity in your family and church. Psalm 133:1-3, Acts 4:32-36

Day 15 Ask God for the outpouring of the Holy Spirit. Joel 2:28-32, Acts 2:1-13

Day 16 Pray for God's divine protection and fresh anointing upon your biological and spiritual parents. Psalm 91:1-16, Psalm 92:10

Day 17 Pray for the success and accomplishment of your goals for this year. Acts 19:11-19, Acts 2:47

Day 18 Ask God for the wind of change in your favour. Genesis 8:1-5, Numbers 11: 31-32, Psalm 147:18

Day 19 Pray for the stability and growth of your children. Isaiah 54:13-17, Luke 1:80, Luke 2:52

Day 20 Ask God for the grace to overcome every obstacle and impossibilities in your pathway. Luke 1:37, Zechariah 4:6-10

Day 21 Give thanks to God for answered prayers. Psalm 3:4, Colossians 1;12-14

The Most Important Question of Your Life

WHAT WILL HAPPEN TO YOU WHEN YOU DIE?

If you are unsure of the answer to this question, or if you are afraid you will not spend eternity in heaven, there's good news for you. The Bible says:

> *"For God so loved the world that He gave His only begotten Son, that whoever believes in Him should not perish but have everlasting life."*
>
> John 3:16

Because God loves and values you so much, He made a way for you to be saved. He sent His Son, Jesus Christ, to die so mankind could be redeemed from sin.

The Bible also says concerning salvation:

> *"Jesus answered and said unto him, "Most assuredly, I say to you, unless one is born again, he cannot see the kingdom of God."*
>
> John 3:3

Salvation does not come from following a certain religion, doing good deeds, or living a good moral life. The Bible says there is only one way to receive salvation.

You must be born again by accepting Jesus Christ as your Saviour. Settle this most important question of your life! I want you to join me now in praying this prayer for salvation.

Don't just read it; make a conscious effort to speak these words from the very depths of your being. When you finish this prayer, you will be born again:

Dear God,

I come to you in the Name of Jesus. You said in your Word that "If I confess with my mouth the Lord Jesus and believe in my heart that God has raised Him from the dead, I will be saved." **para -Romans 10:9**. *I believe in my heart that Jesus Christ is the Son of God. I believe He was raised from the dead for my justification. Your word says, "For with the heart one believes unto righteousness, and with the mouth confession is made unto salvation."* **Romans 10:10**. *I do believe with my heart, and I now confess with my mouth that Jesus is my Lord. Therefore I am saved!*

Thank you Lord!

WELCOME TO THE FAMILY OF GOD!

Congratulations! If you have prayed this prayer sincerely from your heart, then the Bible says you are now saved!

Receiving Jesus Christ as Saviour and Lord was the right decision. You are now a child of God, a friend of Jesus and a true Christian. God now dwells in you and wants to nurture His relationship with you. You have an exciting time ahead of you! You will learn and experience many new things. There will be times of trial and temptation - but do not fear. Jesus promised He would never leave you nor forsake you **(Hebrews 13:5).**

For your relationship with Jesus Christ to develop and grow, communication with Him is necessary. That is done mainly as you pray and read the Bible. If you do not have a Bible and don't know where to get one, please use my contact details to request your free copy of the Bible.

No doubt you may have many questions too. Be assured that there are answers. However, you cannot expect to get them all answered today! Just as a young child cannot understand everything, so you may need to learn and grow, before you will be able to comprehend some things.

Finally, find a Bible-based Church. There you can praise and worship God, learn more of God and His Word, and find fellowship with other Christians. Please write me and let me know that you just received Jesus into your life and I will be glad to send you some helpful materials.

Remember, Jesus loves you and He will never forsake you!

Commendations
'The Making of a Father'

This is a brilliant study of a topical issue, especially as our homes and, indeed, societies are becoming deficient of quality fathers who can make positive impact. The book touches on the major gaps that have resulted in the erosion of quality values from our private and public life. It is a book that is well written and carefully woven together. This is a compulsory reading for every father and for everybody who aspires for position of leadership.

Dr. Abiodun Alao

Pastor Paul has written about God moving in his spirit to lead him from stage to stage in becoming a 'father'. He pursues this calling of being a 'father' to many Christians in his church today.

As a 'father' he guides and leads them as the Spirit leads him.

The book describes the way God has been in each stage of the process of learning to be a 'father', and has revealed to him how he must change and adapt new ideas at each stage. God Himself is the author of the changes and Pastor Paul merely describes in this book what God did in his life.

However the information may be helpful to other Christians. It may help them to grow and mature and learn to be 'fathers' themselves. But we must remember every person is an individual and God deals with each one of us differently according to our different personalities.

This book is a helpful guide to seeing God act in someone's life.

D.J. Maclennan

The Making of a Father is a book that stood out among many books with a unique revelation of the mind of God concerning fatherhood.

"....It takes a mature man to put his dream aside for others..." the most catching phrase that Bishop Paul had used to truly expose my mind to understand why everything changed when I became a father....and if I had read this book before embarking on fatherhood, I would have managed the change better. The in-depth use of food technology in this book as a metaphorical exposition is really "cool." The making of a father is easy to read and simple to understand, an eye opener and a revealer of a deep truth about the part of a man that is rarely discussed.

The book allows me to assess where I am in the process, as much as it allows me to know what is yet to be expected as I come into the fullness of fatherhood. I think every man, especially most male young adults will be well prepared and equipped for fatherhood if they get to read this book before getting into the process.....

It is mind blowing – a reflection of the person of my Bishop

Dr. Victor Olusegun Aigbogun

References

1 US Census Bureau, Population Division, 2010 http://www.census.gov/popest/

2 World Bank World development indicators, 2011
http://data.worldbank.org/data-catalog/world-development indicators

3 Oxford Online Dictionary

4 Kouzes, J & Posner,B (2003)
Credibility: How Leaders Gain and Lose It, Why People Demand It.

Servant Leadership Quotes Trinity Western University

http://twu.ca/academics/graduate/leadership/servant-leadership/quotes.html